Loved

*"Come to me,
all you who are weary and burdened,
and I will give you rest.*

*Take my yoke upon you and learn from me,
for I am gentle and humble in heart,
and you will find rest for your souls.*

For my yoke is easy and my burden is light."

Jesus as recorded in Matthew 11:28-30 (NIV)

Loved

WOMEN WHO FOUND HOPE AND HEALING IN JESUS
A narrative Bible study

Their Stories

Narrated by

A. Sue Russell with Médine Keener

CROSS
PERSPECTIVES
Whittier, California

Cross Perspectives
Whittier, California

crossperspectives@gmail.com

Scripture translations within the narrations are provided by the author. Other Scripture quotations are taken from the King James Version of the Bible unless noted with (NIV) which are taken from the Holy Bible, New International Version®, NIV®. Copyright ©1973, 1978, 1984, 2011 by Biblica, Inc.™ Used by permission of Zondervan. All rights reserved worldwide. www.zondervan.com The "NIV" and "New International Version" are trademarks registered in the United States Patent and Trademark Office by Biblica, Inc.™

Cover and graphics by David Russell

Printed in the United States of America
2020619
Names: Russell, A. Sue | with Keener, Médine,
Title: Loved, Women Who Found Hope and Healing in Jesus, / A. Sue Russell ; with Médine Keener.
Description: Whittier, California : Cross Perspectives, 2018 | Narratives of encounters between women and Jesus that integrate insight from Scriptural texts and background information and apply them to practical situations today.
Identifiers: ISBN 978-1-64047-005-7 (soft-cover) | ISBN 978-64047-001-9 (epub)
Library of Congress Control Number: 2018953868
CrossPerspectives, Whittier, CA

Dedicated to
those who seek to bring
hope and healing
through Jesus' love

Table of Contents

An Invitation

*"Come to me
all you who are weary and burdened
and I will give you rest."*

Matthew 11:28 (NIV)

"Then will you let me plant the seed of Love now?" asked the Shepherd.

Much-Afraid shrank back. "I am afraid," she said, "I have been told that if you really love someone you give them the power to hurt and pain you in a way no one else can."

"That is true," agreed the Shepherd, "To love does mean to put yourself into the power of the loved one and to become very vulnerable to pain

and you are very Much-Afraid of pain are you not?"

She nodded miserably and then said shamefacedly, "Yes, very much afraid of it." …

"The seed looks very sharp," she said shrinkingly. "Won't it hurt if you put it into my heart?"

He answered gently, "It is so sharp that it slips in very quickly. But Much-Afraid, I have warned you that Love and Pain go together, for a time at least. If you would know love, you must know pain too."[1]

This book is an invitation. It is an invitation to the bruised and beaten. To the lonely, the depressed, the hurting. To those who have been used and tossed away. To those who have wounds so deep, losses so painful you are unable to face them.

This book is an invitation to begin a journey of healing. A journey that is painful and long. But a journey that leads to life and love.

Some of you have been on that journey for a long time. You are weary and exhausted and wondering if it's worth it. You have been walking a path to the top of a mountain and thought you were almost there. Then as you turned the corner you saw the end of your journey was still a long way off.

You are tired and discouraged. You're not sure you are ready to go on. You're ready to quit. This book is an invitation to come rest a while and reflect how far you've come.

Some of you have not yet begun the journey. You are afraid that you might be asked to do something that you can't do. You are afraid you will add one more failure, one more hurt to the many wounds you have already. Fear keeps you from starting. You are not sure if it's worth the pain.

But I want to congratulate you. You have taken a first step. You have picked up this book and have read up to here. That in itself took courage.

This book is an invitation to trust again.

Healing cannot occur without relationship.

This book invites you to meet a man who is different. A man who is like no one else. A man who is Love.

This man treated women with dignity, respect, and love. He reached down and met them where they were. He got involved in their lives. This book is an invitation to meet the women who were touched by his love and began to live and love again.

But most of all, this book is an invitation to love and be loved. It is an invitation to live. Living in this world we will experience pain, but the journey to love often passes through pain. This is an invitation to start. An invitation to allow your life to be transformed by love.

Reflection Questions

An Invitation

This chapter invites you to begin a journey of healing.

1. How do you define a journey of healing?

2. What are some of your hopes for this journey?

3. What are some concerns as you consider starting this journey?

4. What are some barriers blocking you from starting this journey?

5. What would you like Jesus to do for you?

The Journey – Part 1
Held Captive

Luke 4:18-19

The Spirit of the Lord is upon me, because
he hath anointed me to preach the gospel to the poor;
he hath sent me to heal the brokenhearted,
to preach deliverance to the captives,
and recovering of sight to the blind,
to set at liberty them that are bruised,
To preach the acceptable year of the Lord.

1
The Fighter

The Canaanite Woman

Mark 7:24-30, Matthew 15:21-28

Her face was lined with determination. A fierce pride. Her life was a constant struggle. Often she felt beaten, but she refused to give up. For her daughter's sake she would keep fighting.

Her husband had left her when their daughter was four months old. With no family, no marketable skills, she raised her daughter as best she could. She refused to become a prostitute, one of the few means of earning money for unskilled women. Her daughter might have to live with the shame of not having a father but she would not live with the shame of a mother who was a prostitute.

She worked long hours in fields, her daughter sitting quietly in the shade while she worked. Although her days were filled with labor, they were filled with joy. The laughter of her daughter, turning even the darkest nights into joy, comforted her and gave her the courage to keep fighting.

But now the light had gone out. Her daughter was sick, very sick. Not a sickness that could be cured by physicians. The foaming at the mouth, the cutting, the biting, the agony. Her daughter was demon possessed. For this sickness there was no hope.

Or was there? The town was buzzing with rumors about a man who had just arrived. A rabbi, a Jewish teacher. Rumors were spreading of how even the demons were subject to his command. Some said that the Jewish dream for a Messiah, the Son of David, had come to pass. He had come, the savior of the Jews. But who was she? A Jewish rabbi would not even listen to her—a woman, even worse, a Gentile woman. She was less than a dog in the eyes of the Jews. How could she expect him to help?

She didn't care. She knew what she must do. She would not let her daughter die. She didn't care what it took. Quickly grabbing a shawl, she set out to find this man. From person to person she went, asking if they had seen the Jewish rabbi. But for all the commotion his arrival had caused, no one knew where he was staying.

She was frantic with despair. Had he already left? Would she ever find him? Then she glimpsed two strangers in the market place. Perhaps they had come with the rabbi. Perhaps they would know where he was staying.

"Please tell me where the teacher is staying," she cried as she met them in the street. "My daughter is dying. Please, he can heal her." The disciples kept walking, ignoring her, intent on completing the errands Jesus had asked them to do.

But the woman kept following them shouting, "Please, my daughter is dying. Please tell your teacher. I just want a moment of his time. Just a moment. Please, just let me ask."

"How are we going to get rid of this Gentile dog?" said one disciple under his breath to the other. "Jesus was sent to us Jews. His ministry is among us. Who does she think she is anyway?" They kept walking, ignoring her pleas, making their way back to where they were staying. They assumed she would tire of waiting and leave.

As the two men entered the courtyard, the woman stood outside the gate staring, bewildered, heartbroken—but only for a moment. With renewed determination she ran through the courtyard and through the door where she saw men lingering, listening.

The disciples caught up with her just as she entered the room where Jesus was talking with his disciples. As they took her by the arms to lead her out of the room, she shouted,

"Lord, Son of David, have mercy on me! My daughter is suffering greatly from being demon possessed!"

Stunned silence fell on the room as the disciples stared at the woman. The disciples, suddenly embarrassed and ashamed, nervously tried to explain, "Master, we couldn't stop her. We tried to ignore her, but she kept crying after us and followed us here. Send her away!"

Jesus looked from the woman to his disciples. The woman who was determined to have her daughter healed. The disciples whose prejudice would stop her. All around the room Jesus saw contempt and hatred for this woman. Hearts in silent agreement. Yet none brave enough to voice their words.

Jesus turned back to the woman and voiced the thoughts of every man in that room, "I was sent only to the lost sheep of Israel." Silently the disciples applauded Jesus' answer. That told her. Now she'll leave.

The woman lifted her eyes to his as he spoke. She was met not with hate, but with love. Love that told her that this was not his answer but theirs. Love that gave her the courage, the determination to keep fighting. Instead of a rebuff, his words were an invitation. Slowly she walked to where he was sitting and knelt before him. Keeping her eyes only on him she pleaded, "Lord, help me."

A smile began to play on the corner on his lips. He liked the determination of this woman. A fighter, she was not going to give up until she had what she came for. Like a father affectionately teasing a child, he gently challenged her. "It is not right to take the children's bread and toss it to the dogs."

Silently the disciples cheered. That told her. Their smug looks indicated that they all knew Jesus was telling the woman that he would only be helping the Jews, not the Gentiles.

But the woman had seen the smile forming on Jesus' lips. She knew she had won. . . With a glimmer in her eye she accepted his challenge and replied, "Yes, Lord, but even the little puppies eat the crumbs that fall from their master's table."

Jesus laughed. Not so much from the woman's answer but from the stunned look on his disciples' faces. They had been set up. The disciples looked downward, unwilling to meet Jesus' eyes. They were ashamed of their unmasked prejudice. Jesus not only welcomed but enjoyed bantering with this woman. They had only seen a Gentile woman; Jesus had seen a person of worth and determination.

Jesus once again looked at the woman with eyes full of love, admiration, and respect, "Woman you have great faith. Your request has been granted."

The fighter had beaten the odds. When the world said there was no hope, she dared to hope. When the world said she had no right to ask, she asked anyway. When the world said there was no way, she found a way—The Way.

I believe that God has a special place in his heart for the fighter. The person who beats all odds to be healed. The person who doesn't listen to facts and figures but listens to a God who responds. People who stand boldly before God and won't let go until God blesses them:

Abraham, who asked God if there were but fifty righteous people would He save a whole city. And dared to continue asking until he was satisfied his nephew Lot and his family would be saved.

Moses, who boldly said to God, "Show me your glory" and God did.

Jacob who would not let go until God blessed him.

Peter, who did not let his failure defeat him but sought out the One who could restore him.

The blind man sitting on the edge of the road shouting, "Son of David, have mercy upon me." The crowd told him to "shut up." Jesus told him, "Come here."

The fighter. The single parent who struggles to be both mom and dad to a child. Who struggles to stay out of poverty, to give her child a chance in the world.

The fighter. The person abused as a child, struggling with deep emotional wounds. The world calls them victims and survivors. God calls them more than conquerors.

The fighter. The pregnant teen. The world says avoid the shame, get rid of it, you have your rights. The church condemns them, marks them. An example of a good kid gone bad. Keep them away from influencing our kids. God says, "Yes, you made a wrong choice but keep fighting. We'll work this out together."

The fighter. The addict. She tries and fails. She struggles with urges. Her body says to give in to them, give up. God says, "Get up, don't give up. You don't fail until you fail to try again."

There is a bold persistence in a fighter. They will probably fail as many times as they succeed, but they get up and try again. There is a special beauty in a hard fought faith.

There are times when healing comes instantly. Many times Jesus answered the pleas of people at their first request or even sought them out. But there are times when he did not answer so quickly. God's answer to our prayers, to His promises, are not always according to our timetable.

How many years was it between Joseph's dreams and when his brothers bowed before him? How many years was it between Moses' calling and the Israelites' first footsteps out of Egypt? How many years was it between David's anointing and his crowning as king?

Often when we begin our journey of healing, we expect an afternoon stroll. Or at least that is what we want. We want healing to be short, quick, and painless. Most of all we want it to be over so we can get on with life.

We'll try various suggestions, read various books, try various methods in our search for healing. If one method doesn't work we'll try another. I'm not saying those things are wrong. But often we bounce from one thing to another because we think there must be an easier way. If we're really honest with ourselves, we have to admit that we are actually looking for a way to be healed without pain.

With emotional healing there are no easy answers. There is no quick fix or painless path. Unfortunately the only way to healing is through pain. Often we would like to somehow remove that step from the healing process. The sooner we accept that pain is part of the process, the sooner we will learn to embrace it, grow from it, learn to accept it as a friend.

We also would like something else or someone else to 'fix' us. But no one can fight the battle for us. They can stand in the corner and cheer us on. They can pick us up when we get knocked down. But they cannot fight for us. They cannot take the pain away. We must face the pain.

If a butterfly is not allowed to struggle out of its cocoon, it will not live. It is in the struggling that its wings reach their full development.

The problem with some methods, books, and people is they offer easy answers. Too easy. These desperately offer to help a person out of their spiritual cocoon and try to make the healing process as painless as possible. We want the person to be free, to know what it is like to fly. So we simplify the healing process. Follow these procedures. Pray these steps, and you will be healed. You will be able to get on with life.

Sometimes these shortcuts look tempting. We get tired of struggling. Just when we think we are finally healed, we find ourselves once again in pain. How tempting it is to try a method and then be able to say, "I'm healed. I'm free," and then simply get on with life.

But if our cocoon is cut away too soon, if we never have to struggle, we will never be healed. We will never be able to fly. If we try to move on to a step prematurely in our healing, confront a perpetrator, get involved in ministry, we may never face our pain. Thinking we are healed of our past we may no longer face it. And although we may have made it out of our cocoon, we will never really be free.

But if we are willing to face the pain, if we are determined to keep fighting we will not be alone. Jesus himself promises that he will never leave us or forsake us. He will walk with us until we are finally free.

Reflection Questions
Chapter 1 - The Fighter

1. What or who are you fighting for?

2. Why is your fight worth fighting?

3. What are some barriers that you face?

4. How do you see yourself?

5. How do you think Jesus sees you?

6. What in your fight are you struggling with right now?

7. Who might be willing to walk with you through your pain?

2
When Dreams Die

He was dead. Her only son, the only heir of her husband. Not long ago they had been a family. Her son's laughter frequently echoed in the security of a loving home. Through their love they had taught him to love others and to love God.

They had dreamed together. A trip to Jerusalem when he was of age. The girl he would marry. The day when he would be old enough to work alongside his father.

He had shown a natural aptitude for carpentry. She remembered the days when he would rush in and show her his latest creation. A roughly planed handle or a crooked chair. Her husband inevitably sauntered in, standing behind him, eyes glowing with pride.

Then her husband had died. Suddenly he was gone. One moment he was in her arms. The next day he was in the grave. In one moment their family was ripped apart. In one moment all of their dreams had died.

Her son was only twelve then. How bravely he had entered a man's world too soon. He worked long and hard as an apprentice. Soon he would have his own shop. And soon a bride.

She had begun to dream again. A house, a home. The special room just for her. The grandchildren she would look after. They would be family again.

But now he was gone. Friends had come to comfort her, but there could be no comfort. She felt she had cried her last tear when her husband died, but now pain pierced her heart once again.

She sat with him, alone, one last time. She looked upon his face, now ashen with death, trying to memorize the features she would see no more. In quiet despair she released him, her dreams, her hope, to her only Hope. Even as she faced a life of extreme poverty, she placed her trust in the Lord, her Lord. Echoing the words of another who had lost all he had, she quietly said, "The Lord gave, and the Lord has taken away. May the name of the Lord be praised." She let her dreams die.

There was a gentle touch on her shoulder as the men came to carry the body to the grave. Bravely she walked beside the open bier as it was carried to the city gates. Deep in her private thoughts, she never noticed the approach of the stranger.

Suddenly the funeral procession stopped. She looked up to meet the eyes of a young rabbi. His eyes seemed to look into her very soul and feel her pain. There was such a depth of understanding in his eyes. She began to weep once more.

"You don't need to cry anymore," Jesus said quietly. He walked over to the bier and touched the young man.

Slowly there was movement from the bier. The body, that had been a corpse a moment ago, sat up. The facecloth fell off, and the young man opened his eyes. "Where am I? Who are you? Why am I all tied up?"

The men carrying the bier were stunned. Mouths gaping, they stood shocked. Slowly they put down the bier and backed away. Jesus smiled at their expressions and released the young man from his grave clothes. Taking the young man by the hand, he gave him back to his mother.

Dreams die. The dream of a happy marriage. The dream of children turning back to the Lord. The dream of a happy childhood. The dream of being healed, finally free from inner struggles.

Ever since sin entered the world, dreams have died. The very first family was shattered when one brother killed another. Sometimes through no fault of our own, our dreams are shattered.

We would like to blame God when dreams die. We shake our fist at God for taking away our dream. We think if we are just good enough, use the right words, say the right prayer, make a bargain, we can manipulate God into giving back our dream. And when He does not, we walk away from Him saying He does not care.

But He does care. Life is not always as God would choose it to be for us. But God allows humans to make their own choices. Unfortunate choices. Evil choices. Self-serving choices. God does not intervene to stop someone from destroying another's dream, but He does promise to give us new ones, better ones.

We have to let go of our broken dreams. But it requires trust to let go of a dream, even a broken one. How can a person who has never learned to trust, begin to trust when it seems as though God allowed dreams to become broken, forgotten, unfulfilled? How can we trust in a God who does not seem to care?

We can't. Trust must be learned. People learn about trusting God through trusting people. Scripture, prayers, procedures will not always help a person learn to trust. To let go of a dream, we have to be convinced reality isn't so bad. That requires a relationship with a real person, more than can be accomplished in a two-hour appointment or with pat answers.

Trust requires a long-term commitment. Consistency, transparency, authenticity. A relationship in which no matter what happens, we will not be rejected. A safe place to let go of broken dreams. Through people we learn to trust in a God who cares, who loves us, who keeps His promises.

And when our hands are finally open, sometimes God gives our dreams back. Unexpectedly. Instantly. The son brought back to life. The mother instantly healed from addiction. The family reunited. In one moment reality becomes immeasurably better than we could ever hope or imagine in even our wildest dreams.

For others, dreams are resurrected in a process through pain. Healing is a slow struggle, but finally one day we are free. The husband repents and returns to his wife and family. The daughter gets treatment for alcoholism. After a long wait, the prodigal comes back. It seems as though there is even greater rejoicing when the victory is through pain.

But what about when God does not seem to answer our prayers? We pray. We struggle. But God doesn't seem to take away our desires. We dream of being healed, but the wounds are so deep there will always be scars. Sometimes, for reasons we do not understand, God does not give us back our dreams.

For some, longings are never fulfilled. We do not get married, we never have a child, never regain our family. And for others, life is so difficult they cannot even begin to dream what it would be like to have a day of refuge, a day with enough to eat, a day without hunger. What about their dreams?

But God never promised we would get our dreams back, at least here on earth. God promises something better. A place where dreams will never die. Heaven.

Jesus' resurrection sealed that promise forever. No matter what evil people do on earth they cannot take away that dream. The resurrection promises that though we experience pain now, God will comfort us. The resurrection reassures us that though we struggle now, soon we will be free.

Heaven. All creation awaits it. A place where dreams do not die. A place where every tear will be erased, forever. Every dream we have ever dreamed, every longing of our heart will be fulfilled the moment we look into Jesus' face. Instantly. Gloriously. Triumphantly.

Reflection Questions
Chapter 2 - When Dreams Die

1. Why are dreams important for people?

2. What dreams have died in your life?

3. How have you mourned the loss of your dreams?

4. What dreams do you still have that remain unfulfilled?

5. What hope does God give us about our dreams?

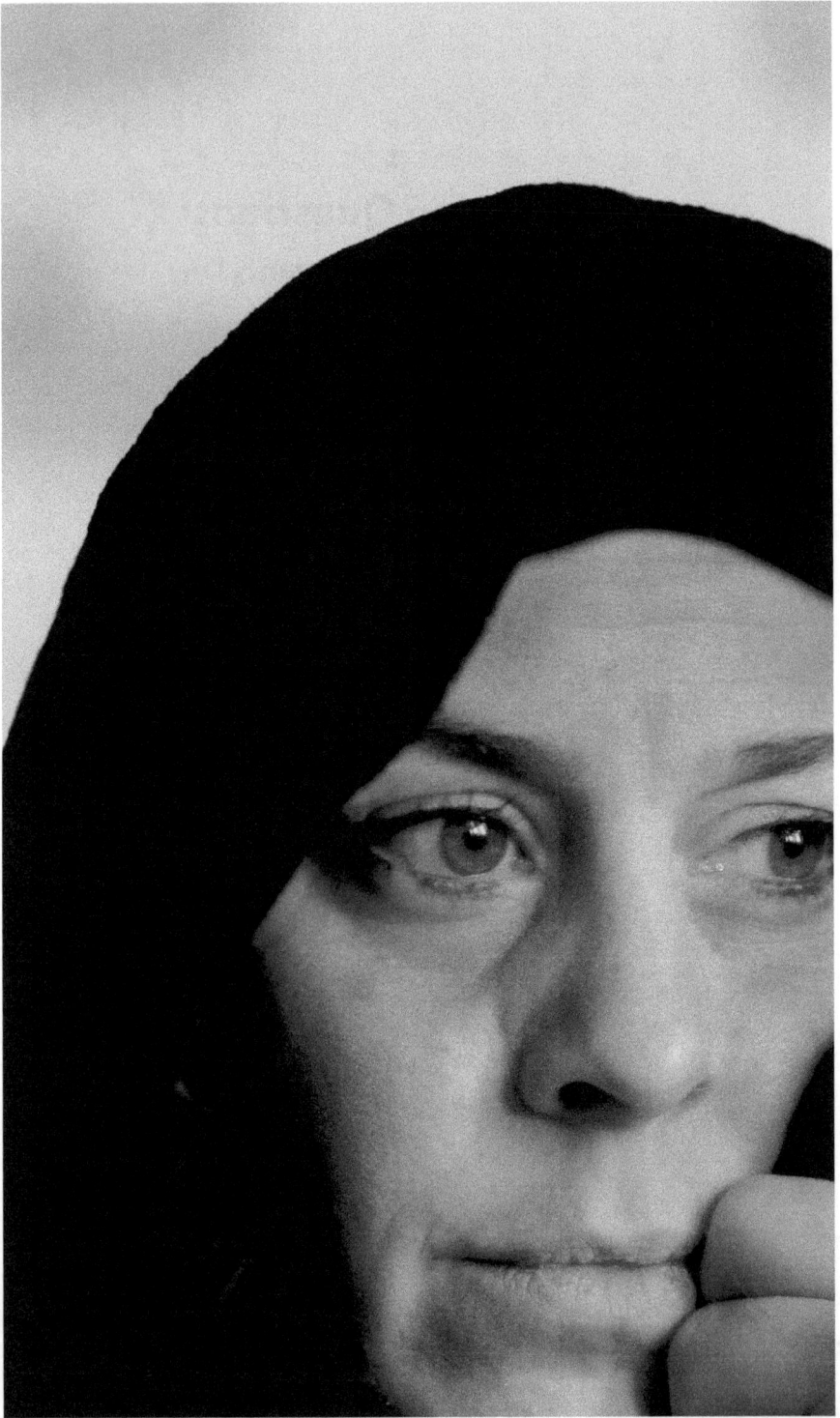

3
Shame Removed

The Woman Bleeding

Mark 5:24-34, Matthew 9:18-26, Luke 8:40-48

Hoping to remain hidden, suddenly the crowd was upon her. He was leaving town. How she had hoped that she could talk to him. To unburden her heart to him. Something in his eyes, in his voice, made her hope that he could heal her.

Twelve years ago it started…the bleeding. Twelve years ago she became unclean…she could not touch her husband, lest he become unclean…she could not cook for her family lest they become unclean.

She had tried everything she could do to make herself clean again. She prayed. She obeyed every command. Yet God had not healed her. She went to one physician after another seeking a cure, only to have her money taken without healing received. Sometimes a treatment would help, and she would have hope. But then the bleeding started again. All the money she had managed to save was now gone.

She had lost her money, her husband, her family, her community. Destitute, isolated, alone. Shame was her only companion.

Where was her God now? The God of Israel. How could He let this happen? Would she, could she, ever be acceptable in His sight again? Would she ever be clean? Or did he, too, look upon her with disgust?

She had her answer. Unclean. Untouchable. Unworthy. An outcast. Surely this was God's judgment for some sin she had committed.

For twelve years she had lived in this isolation. For twelve years she had carried her burden of shame. Alive, yet dead. Separated from God, separated from family, separated from everyone she loved. If only she could be cured, then perhaps she could live again.

She had no hope. If she could not be cured, she would never be clean.

He was leaving now. The whole crowd pressed around her. She knew she shouldn't be there for she was unclean and all those who touched her were unclean. But he was so close, if only, if only....

Lunging forward she managed to touch the edge of his robe. Instantly she knew she was healed. She turned to leave, hoping to remain unnoticed. Suddenly there was a commotion in the crowd.

"Who touched me?" the young rabbi asked, glancing around the crowd. Those immediately surrounding him denied touching him. The woman cowered, trying to remain unseen.

Jesus' disciples, anxious to move on, replied, "Master, the people are crowding and pressing around you. Lord, there are a thousand people touching you. Why do you ask 'Who touched me?'"

Jesus ignored their comment and said, "Someone touched me. I know that power has gone out of me." He continued to look around the crowd until his eyes met the woman who had touched him. Gently his eyes invited her to come to him.

The woman stood for a moment, trembling, not knowing what to do. Would he publicly rebuke her? Would he reject her? His love compelled her to go to him. Her fear held her back. Slowly she moved forward.

The people parted to let her pass and then backed away when they saw who it was. She felt their glares upon her back as she made her way through the crowd.

When she reached Jesus she fell to his feet, trembling, sobbing, waiting for the rebuke she felt sure to come. Gently Jesus knelt in front of her, looking at her with compassion. Without looking up, she told him everything. Her bleeding, her search for a cure, her hopelessness.

"And then," she continued sobbing, "I touched you. I was desperate and did not know what else to do. I wanted to be clean, whole again. I touched you, and I was healed."

When she had finished, she waited in silence for his rebuke, his rejection. Slowly she lifted her eyes to Jesus and saw compassion, love, acceptance. Instead of condemnation, she found forgiveness. He knew her shame and did not reject her.

Jesus took her by the hand and raised her to her feet. In a voice loud enough for the crowd to hear, he spoke to her, "Daughter, you are healed because you have believed in me. You can now go in peace."

Daughter. He had called her daughter. A term of endearment, affection, acceptance. Released from her prison of isolation, she could go in peace.

Peace. Freed from shame at last. Peace with herself. Peace with God. Peace with others.

Shame. A feeling of worthlessness that won't go away. Unacceptable, unloved, unclean…perhaps through no fault of our own. A rape, domestic violence, molestation, sex trafficking, or just being a woman.

Shame that says we deserve what life has given us. Shame that says we will never be acceptable, that we must hide from others and even from God.

Shame starts with a lie. You are worthless, you deserve it, you will never be whole again. You don't deserve to be loved. We believe it. We accept it. It becomes who we are. Shame becomes our companion. Shame becomes a disease that many people carry and few ever heal.

Shame leads us to act out who we believe we are. Deep sorrow leads to repentance, but living in shame becomes a vicious cycle. We go from one failure to another. Each failure reinforcing the lie: "You will not amount to anything. You are worthless."

The kind of pain that shame brings is messy pain. Pain that only leads to greater destruction and death. When the pain becomes too great to bear, we give up on life.

The only way to break that cycle is through truth. The truth about ourselves from God's perspective and from others. But the only way we can begin to believe that truth is when it is reflected in other people through grace. Love that says no matter what I've done you will still accept me. I can show you the worst dragons I have hidden in the dungeon of my soul and you will still love me.

Love allows me to live without 'shoulds' and 'oughts.' Love allows me to just be me. I can be content with the person God created me to be. With gratitude I can accept my gifts. With humility I can accept my weaknesses. Love lets me be, well, human.

Love does not look at what I have done. It looks at who I am. Lovable, cherished because I was created that way. I do not have to do anything to become lovable. I have value. I am lovable. I don't have to earn it. Period!

Love sees beyond the actions and looks at the person. Love sees beyond the brokenness, the failures, the humiliations and restores dignity. Love sees beyond the broken pieces and sees a vessel of honor.

Moses murdered an Egyptian yet grace saw the leader who would lead the people of Israel out of Egypt.

King David committed adultery, then lied and arranged a murder to cover it up. Yet love still called him a man after God's own heart.

Rahab was a prostitute when grace found her. Love chose her to be the great, great grandmother of King David.

Paul was a hateful, spiteful man. Love transformed him into the greatest missionary of all times.

Love takes the failures, the mistakes, what people intended for evil and transforms them into good. Love removes shame forever.

Reflection Questions
Chapter 3 - Shame Removed

1. What are sources of shame in your life or in your culture?

2. What shame is keeping you in captivity?

3. What events in the past still keep you hiding from others?

4. How has your shame kept you isolated?

5. What do you believe about yourself that love says is not true?

6. How do you think God sees you?

7. How would really understanding God's love for you change your life?

Held Captive

To Set the Prisoners Free

Matthew 11:28-30 (NIV)

"Come to me,
all you who are weary and burdened,
and I will give you rest.
Take my yoke upon you and learn from me,
for I am gentle and humble in heart,
and you will find rest for your souls.
For my yoke is easy and my burden is light."

4
Liberated by Love

Mary and Martha

Luke 10:38-42

Martha stood at the window looking across the fields, re-membering. In her mind she could see her siblings Mary and Lazarus as children running, playing tag across the field. She smiled at how her mother scolded Mary for being such a tomboy.

Mary, only a year older than Lazarus, was his constant companion. Mary...curious, sensitive, a natural learner always found some excuse to be outside the synagogue when Lazarus was learning his lessons. The classes were for boys only, but Mary would always pester Lazarus until he sat down and taught her all he had learned that day.

Martha, ten years older than Mary, was a second mother to her. Even as a child, Martha had always been practical, level-headed. She had always been the responsible one. The one you could count on. The one who knew her duty, what her culture expected of her.

When Martha was just 16, she became Mary's only mother when their parents had died. Since then Martha had managed the household. Until the day when Lazarus would be able to manage his own affairs, she was father and mother to them both.

"Martha, Martha, they're here," shouted Mary, running breathlessly into the kitchen.

Martha broke out of her daydreaming and began to make final preparations for the dinner she was preparing. She loved Jesus and often had him and his disciples over for meals and to rest from their journeys. She dutifully embraced the role expected of women of Israel. She managed the household so that men could fulfill their roles as participants in the spiritual life of Israel. But the servants were gone today, and she had to get everything ready for her unexpected guests.

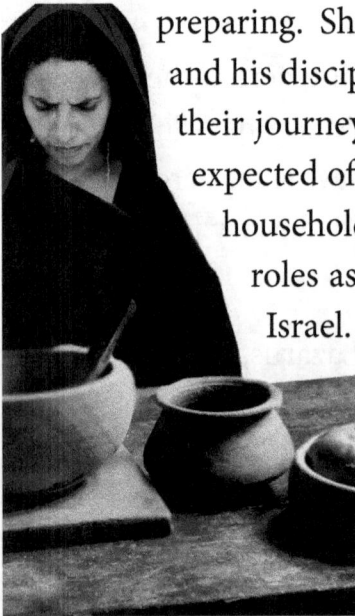

"Quick, Mary, get the water and towels ready so they can wash their feet and then come back for some drinks," ordered Martha. She hastily returned to her preparations for the feast she would serve. Martha just could not serve a simple meal. Hospitality was her calling, and she wanted to serve extravagantly.

"Mary, the drinks are ready," called Martha into the main room. Mary quickly came and got the tray of drinks and began serving Jesus and his disciples. They were talking about the growing controversy surrounding Jesus and his new teachings. She listened quietly as she served. Slowly, Mary served drinks, moving around the group of men until she came to Jesus' side where her brother was sitting.

Jesus began talking about the meaning of love and what it meant to love God with all your heart. Mary was mesmerized and sat beside Lazarus, listening, reflecting. Jesus caught her eye and smiled, welcoming her into the group of his disciples.

In the kitchen Martha had not even noticed Mary's absence. Caught up in the preparations, she frantically rushed around the kitchen. She realized that they needed more water and turned to order Mary to go to the well for more. No Mary. She looked around the kitchen. Pitchers of drinks still waited on the table to be served. The dirty towels lay forgotten.

"Just like Mary. Always the daydreamer," Martha mumbled silently under her breath. "How could it possibly take her that long to serve the drinks? Doesn't she realize how much I have to do? Where is she when I need her?"

"Mary!" Martha shouted. Nothing.

"Maryyyyyy!" Martha shouted as she began walking to where Jesus and his disciples were sitting. Fuming, mumbling under her breath, she entered the room, saw Mary sitting, listening with the disciples. Horrified and embarrassed at the breach of cultural etiquette, she shouted, "Mary!"

An awkward silence filled the room. Every head turned toward Martha. Jesus waited, looking at her, amusement on his face.

Suddenly she was embarrassed, ashamed. Quickly trying to justify her intrusion, she said, "Lord, don't you even care that Mary has left me to do all the work myself? Tell her to help me!" The unspoken message: Teach Mary her appropriate place, in the kitchen where women fulfill their religious duty according to the religious law.

As soon as she had said it, she wished she hadn't. But she was too proud to back down. She was used to having her own way. Martha looked at Jesus defiantly.

A smile played at the corners of Jesus' mouth.

He liked her spirit, her devotion to him. Her desire to serve God with all her heart in the way she had been taught...in the home, in the kitchen, a woman's place. He

44

continued to look into Martha's eyes, searching her heart. Martha looked down, avoiding his searching gaze. Gently he rebuked her, "Martha, Martha. You are so busy with so many things, temporal things. Mary has chosen something better. This will not be taken away from her."

Many times when this story is told, the main point expressed is that Jesus was rebuking Martha because she was busy with too many things. Martha's problem was that she was distracted with her busyness. We need to be like Mary and slow down and listen to Jesus.

That preaches well, but it is not the main lesson of this passage. You see, throughout history and in Jesus' culture, women were considered inferior. They were considered marred, treacherous, deceitful and easily deceived. Many times they were treated as property rather than as persons. They were considered incapable of participating in the intellectual and spiritual life of Israel. Women were marginalized from the public and spiritual life of their communities.

Better for women to be in the home than in the synagogue. Better for women to take care of others' physical needs than their own spiritual and intellectual needs.

Better for women to stay in the back room rather than the front room, let alone a boardroom, classroom, or pulpit.

Martha knew her place, but Jesus invited Mary to participate in a new place.

Jesus declared Mary a capable learner. Jesus declared Mary a person of dignity. Jesus declared Mary an important part of the spiritual life of Israel. Jesus welcomed Mary as a disciple. Jesus welcomed Mary as an equal partner with the men. That day, Mary became a co-learner, a co-follower of Jesus.

Many believe women are inferior. From Homer in the ancient world to men in the modern world, women are considered less than equal. Seen as disposable, many girls are killed before they are ever born or sold as slaves. Seen as inferior, education is unavailable and many cannot even read. Seen as property, women work harder and longer, eat less and die younger. Seen as dangerous, women are beaten and violated.

But Jesus invited Mary to stay…as a person, as a learner, as a disciple. In a culture where women had no voice, Jesus gave them a voice. In a society where women were inferior, Jesus made them equals. In a society where they were told to stay at home, Jesus invited women to "Follow me."

Reflection Questions
Chapter 4 - Liberated by Love

1. What has your culture told you about the role of women?

2. What have other people told you about yourself that keeps you from exercising your gifts?

3. How did Jesus' actions toward women differ from how others in his culture treated women?

4. How did Jesus' actions toward women differ from how others in your culture treat women?

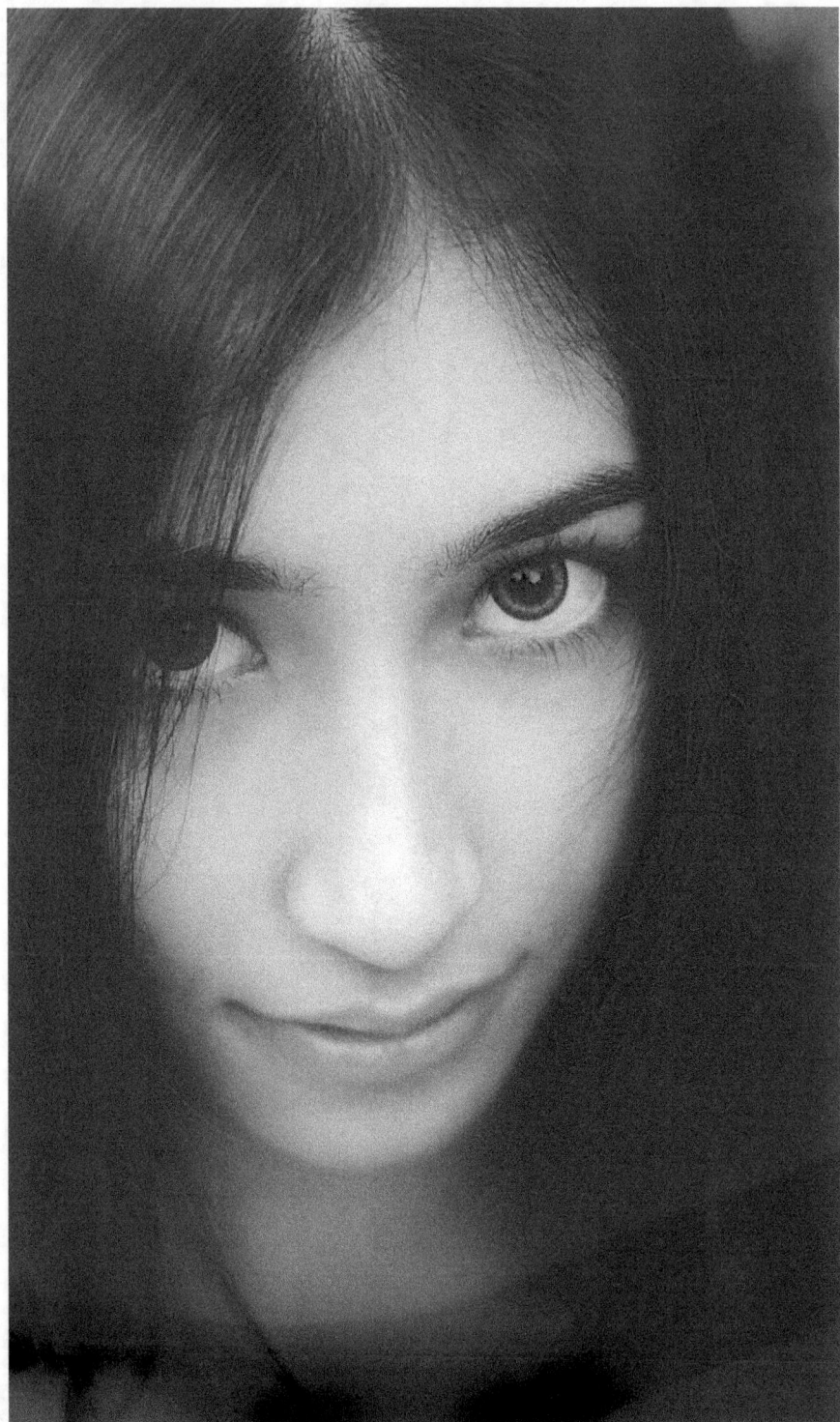

5

Encounter with Truth

The Samaritan Woman

John 4:3-42

She saw him as she approached the well. She knew why he was there. Why would any man be sitting beside the well at noon? She sighed. Why would any woman besides her come to the well at noon? She didn't care what others said. But she came at noon to avoid the gossip and the cold stares.

Her outward bravado hid a deep emptiness in her life. All her life she searched for love. Searched for someone who would cherish her. Fill the deep thirst for love. Five men had promised love. Five men had left her. Five men had taken a part of her from her when they went.

She vowed never to trust a man again. She would live with a man. She had to, how else could she survive? But it would be on her terms.

As she drew closer she recognized from his clothes that he was from Galilee. A Jew. What is a Jew doing here? Jews despised Samaritans. The only person lower than a Samaritan was a woman. Immediately her defenses were up as she arrived at the well.

The young Jewish rabbi smiled as she approached. He looked exhausted from his travels. "Will you give me a drink?" he asked her.

His request completely disarmed her.

Jews would not even sit at the same table as Samaritans, let alone drink from the same cup. Slowly she let down her container into the well, drew it up, and then poured a cup of cold water for this stranger. Her curiosity aroused, she asked boldly, "You are a Jew, but you ask me, a Samaritan woman, for a drink. Why?"

Jesus replied with a smile, "If you knew the gift of God and who I am, you would have asked me to give you living water."

She stared at him. She knew men too well to believe one so easily. Men had told her many things. She wasn't about to believe this one. Especially a Jew. She wouldn't ask anything from a Jew. Yet there was something about him that commanded respect. He was different.

"Sir, you do not have a container to draw water and this well is deep. How are you going to give this living water? This well has been here since the beginning of the nation of Israel. Jacob gave us this well, and it has been used for centuries. Are you claiming to be greater than Jacob?"

Jesus did not take offense at her remark but prolonged her curiosity a little further. He liked the spirit of this woman. He liked her intellect, her curiosity. "Whoever drinks the water in this well will be thirsty again. But whoever drinks the water I give will never be thirsty again. In fact the water I give will give everlasting life."

Who was this man? A rabbi? A teacher? He did not sound like any Jew she had ever met or even like any man she had ever met. He had not come to take, but to give. Her mind still hadn't fully comprehended the meaning of his words. Tentatively she said, "I want this water that you speak of. Give me this water so that I won't have to come here and drink water again."

Jesus looked at her, searching. She did not understand the meaning of his words, or what he was offering. Gently he said, "Go call your husband."

The woman stared at him. Debating, struggling. Jesus waited, watching the inner struggle. She had lied, and

53

deceived and manipulated other men but somehow she could not do so with the man sitting before her. Finally, she told the truth about herself, "I have no husband."

A smile played at Jesus lips as he replied, "That's right." The woman stared at him wide eyed as he continued, "The fact is you have had five husbands and the man you are living with is not your husband."

She stared hard at him. Her heart, her life, her sins were bared open before him. Yet there was no condemnation in his voice. Who was the man who knew the truth about her yet accepted her? He was no ordinary man. Slowly beginning to comprehend, something in her heart stirred. Could he be the prophet, the one who would reveal and restore all things?

"I perceive that you are a prophet," she said, acknowledging his answer. But he was still a Jew and she a Samaritan. Could he be trusted? The Jews will not even let Samaritans worship with them. But who else could this be? Probing further, she stated their historical divide, "Our forefathers worshiped here on the mountain, but the Jews claim the place we must worship is Jerusalem."

Jesus smiled at her question. She was an intelligent woman and had obviously been thinking about these things. Jesus answered her, "You Samaritans really haven't understood who you worship. God has said that salvation will come from the Jews. But the place of worship is no longer important. The time has now come that true worshipers of God will worship in spirit and in truth. God is Spirit, and those who want to worship Him must worship Him in spirit and in truth. These are the worshipers that God seeks."

The woman probed a little further into this man's identity, "I know the Messiah is coming. When he comes he will explain everything to us." *Just like you've done* she thought silently. She waited, intently looking at Jesus. Had she guessed rightly? Is this the One?

Jesus laughed, "Yes, I am the Messiah."

Truth is the beginning of healing. Truth is the beginning, not the end of a relationship with Jesus. Some of us want to hide in a religion instead. Religion allows us to keep truth at a distance, to simply perform the right rituals, say the right words, so that truth never has to come out.

But God does not want religion. He does not want our rituals. He wants us! He wants a relationship with us. He already knows the truth about us. But a true relationship requires us to see the truth about ourselves. Truth hurts. Truth makes us face who we really are. Truth no longer allows us to blame others for our actions. And truth no longer allows us to take responsibility, or blame, for the actions of others.

It is scary to believe the truth. Truth can be uncomfortable. It leaves us naked, exposed, vulnerable. We no longer

55

can hide behind our masks. We have to become responsible. We have to own up to who we are and what we've done.

Truth requires us to accept both the good and bad about ourselves. It means learning to accept that we are not perfect, but we are not totally worthless either. Truth means understanding that our past actions do not have to define us.

Truth will be uncomfortable for a while. We're not used to it. It doesn't feel right. It seems contrary to what we have been told as children by others. But in order to grow, to heal, we have to let go of the lies. We have to acknowledge sin. That is the part that hurts. Growth comes when we begin to accept the truth about ourselves. It is only as we let go of lies and sin that we will be able to see ourselves as God does.

Let me tell you a little story to illustrate this point. There once was a tiny rosebush growing in a field. Just casually passing by, you would not have recognized it as a rosebush. It was a scrawny, thorny little bush, trying to send its roots down into rocky, barren soil. Somehow it had managed to grow on its own with the little rainfall it had received.

A gardener came along one day and spotted the little rosebush. He recognized it as a rare type of rosebush, one that he had longed for all his life. Reaching beyond the thorns he saw that the stalk was hardy enough to transplant. But he would have to wait until the time was right. He knew he could

not rush things or else he might destroy the fragile life that was there.

Finally winter came, and the gardener went to bring the rosebush into his garden. First, he had to prune all the thorny branches that had grown from the years of poor nourishment. Next, he dug carefully around the roots and pruned them as well.

To look at the rosebush right then, you would think that the gardener had destroyed it. All that was left were a few twigs on top and a stub where crooked roots had grown. It looked worse than when it was growing in the rocky soil. Some growth, as thorny as it was, was growth. But now there seemed to be nothing left at all.

The gardener smiled as he carried the rosebush home. He had already dug a hole in preparation and filled it with the best soil and nutrients. Carefully he placed the rosebush

57

into the hole, spreading the short root stubs so they would grow deep.

For a long time the little rosebush did not show any growth. But deep below the surface, the roots were beginning to spread in the good soil, taking in nourishment. Slowly leaves began to grow as the gardener watered and puttered over his little prize plant. And finally one day to the utter delight of the gardener, the little rosebush began to bloom.

Truth begins to prune away the lies we have come to believe. Truth allows sin to be acknowledged and released. It hurts. After all the pruning is done, it seems like there is nothing left. But slowly in the soil of healthy relationships, true friends, helpful mentors, and God's love, we can begin to believe what is really true. And when we begin to believe, we start to become what God has created us to be. True love only flourishes in truth.

Reflection Questions
Chapter 5 - Encounter with Truth

1. What were some barriers between Jesus and the Samaritan woman?

2. What are some barriers between you and Jesus?

3. What truths are you afraid of facing about yourself?

4. What past actions have defined you?

5. How are those truths preventing you from being open with others?

6. What barriers are keeping you from a relationship with God?

7. What are some good things you are afraid to believe about yourself?

6

Encounter with Grace

Woman Caught in Adultery

John 8:2-11

Jesus was sitting, teaching people in the temple courts. Suddenly there was a commotion and a group of Pharisees and teachers of the law came bursting through the crowd, dragging a woman with them. They pushed her forward, directly in front of Jesus and declared, "Teacher, this woman was caught in the very act of adultery. According to the Law of Moses, we are commanded to stone this woman to death. What do you say?"

She stood trembling before him. Ashamed, afraid. Jesus looked around the crowd of men defiantly waiting for him to condemn himself by his actions. Their actions were intended to place him in an impossible dilemma, save this woman or save himself.

There was no doubt the woman was guilty. She had been caught in the very act of adultery. But there was no sign of the man, despite her being caught. Jesus was furious that they would treat this woman as an object to be used for their purposes and then discarded. Bait in a trap. He stared into their faces, searching their hearts. He looked at the woman, compassion filling his heart. He sat. Waiting, searching.

"Tell us, Jesus, tell us what we should do!" The Pharisees were still waiting for an answer. Some were growing uncomfortable as Jesus bent down, writing on the ground.

Finally Jesus stood up. One by one he looked at the men in the crowd. His eyes searching their hearts. One by one the men looked down at the ground. Accused, ashamed. "If any one of you is without sin, then you can be the first to throw a stone at this woman," Jesus said quietly as he once again stooped and wrote on the ground.

One by one those who were present quietly walked away. The older men first. Stones dropped from the hands that moments before were all too ready to throw them. The younger men, seeing the support of their elders was gone, reluctantly left. Finally, only the woman stood before Jesus.

Jesus stood up and looked down at the woman. Gently he asked, "Woman, where are your accusers? Where are those who wish to condemn you? Is there anyone here condemning you?"

For the first time, the woman glanced up. Slowly she looked around her. No one else but Jesus remained. Only stones scattered on the pavement. Gradually comprehending what had happened, she answered, "No one, sir."

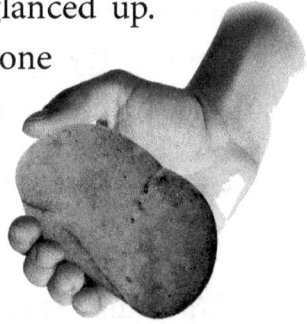

"Neither do I," Jesus replied, "go and sin no more."

I wonder if there are so many abortions because kids are afraid to tell their parents they made a mistake.

I wonder if some of the kids walking in gay rights marches walked away from the church because they could not talk about their inner struggles.

I wonder if people stay away from church because they are afraid they will find stones instead of hugs.

Grace says you made a mistake, let's go on from here.

Grace took the Prodigal from the pigpen and put a robe upon his back and a ring upon his finger. Grace transformed the rebellious son into a loyal son.

Grace found Peter in a fishing boat after his failure and commissioned him to serve. Grace transformed Peter the bragger into Peter the Rock.

Grace found John Mark after he deserted the ship and asked him to try again. Grace transformed the deserter into a faithful servant.

Grace takes in the pregnant teen and gives her a safe, loving environment.

Grace finds the prodigal dying with AIDS and transforms him into a disciple.

Grace finds the child soldier and transforms him into a child of God.

Grace never requires us to be perfect, just obedient. Love allows us to make mistakes and to get up and try again.

Reflection Questions
Chapter 6 - Encounter with Grace

1. What do you think the woman felt like when Jesus forgave her?

2. What kinds of actions do you think are unforgivable?

3. What kinds of choices have you made that you think God cannot forgive?

4. How would your life change if you brought your past failures to God and found forgiveness through Jesus?

The Journey – Part 3

Held Captive

To Set the Prisoners Free

Free, Free at Last

John 8:36

If the Son therefore shall make you free,
ye shall be free indeed.

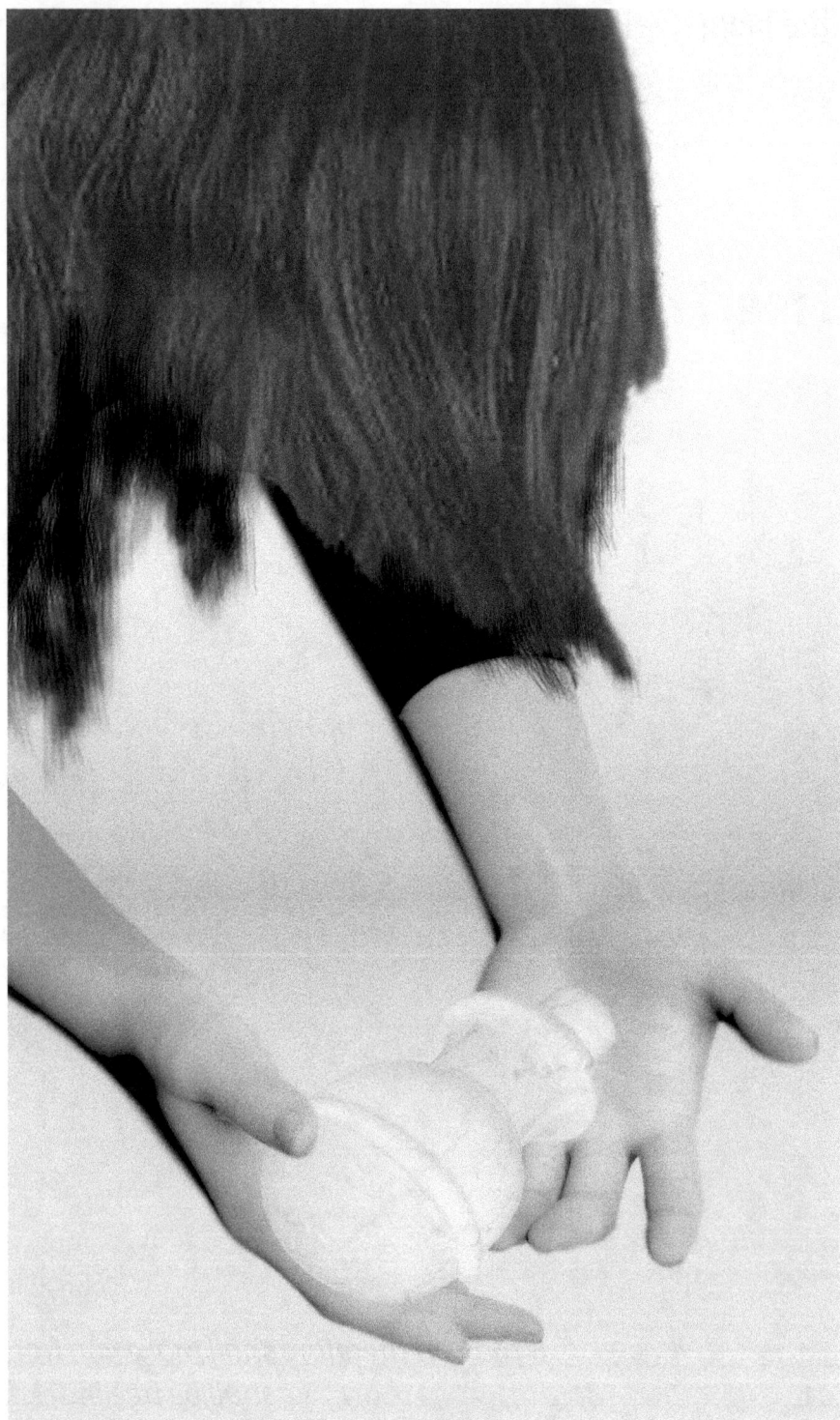

7

Freed To Love

The Sinner

Luke 7:36-50

His look haunted her. Whenever she stopped to think, his words, his voice echoed in her soul. She had tried to ignore him but she felt drawn. She tried to laugh at him, but his words pierced her heart.

He had glanced at her as he taught. In one look he unmasked her facade. She looked honestly at what her life had become. A woman no respectable man would ever be seen with. She smiled for a moment. No, the respectable ones always snuck through the back door. She paced the floor, struggling inwardly. It had not mattered what others thought about her, about her life until he came.

He was different. Somehow he made her want to be different. To be clean. He was like no man she had ever known before. Others had looked at her with lust. He had looked upon her with love, with compassion. She could not stand the struggle any longer. She had to do something. She had to be free.

Quickly grabbing an alabaster jar of perfume, she ran to the house where he was eating. Weeping, broken, tears streaming down her face, she fell at his feet. Not caring what others thought, she let her hair down and began wiping his feet with her hair. She kissed them and anointed them with perfume. Holding them tightly, sobbing, she pleaded, "Oh God, I want to be clean." The prodigal had fallen into the waiting arms of the Father.

Simon, the host and a devout Pharisee, was shocked and speechless. How could Jesus not know who this woman was? How could he even allow such a woman to touch him?

Jesus knew what Simon was thinking. Simon, a religious man who prided himself on his purity, had repulsion written all over his face. Jesus said to Simon, "Two men owned money to a certain moneylender and could not pay it back. One owned him ten times as much as the other, but the moneylender canceled both of their debts. Now who would love him more?"

Simon answered uncertainly, not sure what point Jesus was trying to make, "I suppose the one who owed the most." "That is right," Jesus replied. Then turning to the woman still sobbing at his feet, he continued, "You see this woman, Simon? When I came to your house, you did not provide the customary water so that I could wash my feet. Yet she has wet my feet with her tears and wiped them with her hair. You did not greet me with a kiss, but this woman has not stopped kissing my feet. You did not put oil on my head, but this woman has anointed my feet with oil. Yes, she has sinned much, but the outpouring of her love tonight shows the depth of her repentance. Her many sins are forgiven. Those who do not repent will not experience this forgiveness, they will only love a little."

Speaking softly to the woman, Jesus said, "Your sins are forgiven. Because you have believed in me you are forgiven. Go in peace."

Do you notice the contrast? Here was Simon, a man with high status in his community with all the right religious credentials. Someone you would be glad to have in your church and who probably would be a leader in most churches today. He was someone who looked pretty good in the eyes of the world.

And then there was the woman. We do not know much about her background except that she was a sinner. We do not really know what kind of person she was. All we know is that she was viewed as the wrong kind of person. She was a woman and a sinner. Not someone any respectable person would want to have in their house. Probably not the kind of person most churches want or are comfortable having in the pews.

Two people. One with the best credentials; one with the worst credentials. But it is not who they are that is the focus of the story. It is what they did. Simon, the honorable man, acted dishonorably toward Jesus. He did not even offer Jesus the hospitality of a social equal. Simon treated Jesus as a servant. The woman, the dishonorable woman, honored Jesus in her actions. The right person did the wrong thing, and the wrong person did the right thing. For Jesus, it was the person who did the right thing who he recognized as his follower.

Loving Jesus is not about how you look on the outside. It is about how you respond to Him. One person looked good in the eyes of the world. The other fell before Jesus in full surrender, and she experienced his love, grace, and forgiveness.

Reflection Questions
Chapter 7 - Freed to Love

1. Why do you think the woman came to Jesus?

2. Why do you think Simon reacted the way he did?

3. What was the contrast between Simon's response and the woman's response to Jesus?

4. What was the contrast between Jesus' response to Simon and Jesus' response to the woman?

5. How do we try to look good in the eyes of other people and God?

6. How do we look in the eyes of Jesus?

8

Freed to Praise

The Crippled Woman

Luke 13:10-17

She slowly made her way to the women's section of the synagogue. Crippled, bent over, she moved painfully. For eighteen years she had been this way. For eighteen years she came to praise God.

She did not know why God had allowed this to happen. She loved God. She was devoted to Him. She did not understand His ways, but she was willing to trust, to patiently endure.

She was unable to do much, but she did all that she could. She was loved by all who knew her for her gentle wisdom, her loving manner. Children gathered around listening in delight to her stories. No stranger was ever turned away from her home without a meal. Every week she came to the synagogue, listening intently to God's word. Satan could bind her body, but he could not bind her spirit.

Jesus had seen her come in. His heart was drawn by her devotion. His heart ached for all that she had suffered. She would not suffer one moment longer.

As she looked up from her prayers, he stood and addressed her, "Come up here." Without hesitation she stood and painfully made her way forward. She came before Jesus, bent over, barely meeting his eyes, expectantly waiting. Jesus placed his hands on her shoulders, "Woman, you are set free. You are healed from your suffering."

Immediately she stood up. She lifted her head and looked into Jesus' eyes, tears streaming down her face. "Thank you! Thank you! Thank you!" The woman took Jesus by the hand and began to dance around the synagogue in joy. Praising the Lord in song. Her friends, family, and neighbors who had watched her suffer joined her in her praise. Men, women, and children all joined in and shared her joy. People were laughing and dancing and singing. Exuberant joy, tears of gratitude mingled together.

"STOP!" shouted one of the synagogue leaders, trying to restore order, "STOP!"

People stopped where they were. Silence fell upon the crowd.

"There are six days for work. So you people come and be healed on those days but not on the Sabbath." Rebuked, people only looked down at the floor.

Jesus answered him, "You hypocrites. On the Sabbath each of you unties your ox or donkey so that it can drink water. Then should not this woman, a daughter of Abraham whom Satan had kept bound for eighteen years, be set free on the Sabbath day?"

They stood staring at each other: the leaders, angry at the disruption of their system, and Jesus, angry at their attitude toward this woman, their coldness, their caring more about their religion than they did about people. The leaders, humiliated and ashamed, left the synagogue.

The people stood frozen in place, no one daring to move. Then a voice began to sing praise to God, then another and another until the room was filled with songs of joy, gratitude, and praise.

Grace Busters. They are everywhere. People who are more concerned about doing things according to the rule book than they are about the work God is doing.

Grace Busters. People more concerned with maintaining the system than in getting well. Dysfunctional families that threaten to fall apart when one of the players gets well and refuses to play his or her previous role.

Grace Busters. The family just waiting for the troubled kid to fail again. If the scapegoat in the family gets healed, there is no one to blame for all the problems. There is no one to take away the focus from everyone else's problems.

Grace Busters. The shoulds and oughts of religion. How many people in our churches are trying their best but are bound by religious shoulds and oughts? How many people are crippled and bent over carrying the weight of emotional problems they think that no one will understand? How many people are shackled by hidden desires that they fear people will find out about?

Grace Busters. The eldest son who is upset that the Prodigal gets a party.

Grace Busters. The Pharisees watching Jesus party with the tax collectors.

Perhaps this is why our churches are so joyless. People struggling under the weight of burdens they were never meant to carry. People imprisoned and crippled by secrets they have carried all their life.

Jesus proclaims, "Come to me all you who are weary and heavy laden." To all who are being held captive by thoughts, emotions, hurts, Jesus boldly declares, "I will set you free. Come to me, for I have come so that you will have life, abundant life." Free to live. Free to praise. Free forever.

Reflection Questions
Chapter 8 - Freed to Praise

1. What 'shoulds' and 'oughts' burden you?

2. What expectations of other people cause you to be weary?

3. Who or what are the *Grace Busters* in your life?

4. When have you felt like they quenched your joy?

5. What would abundant life look like for you?

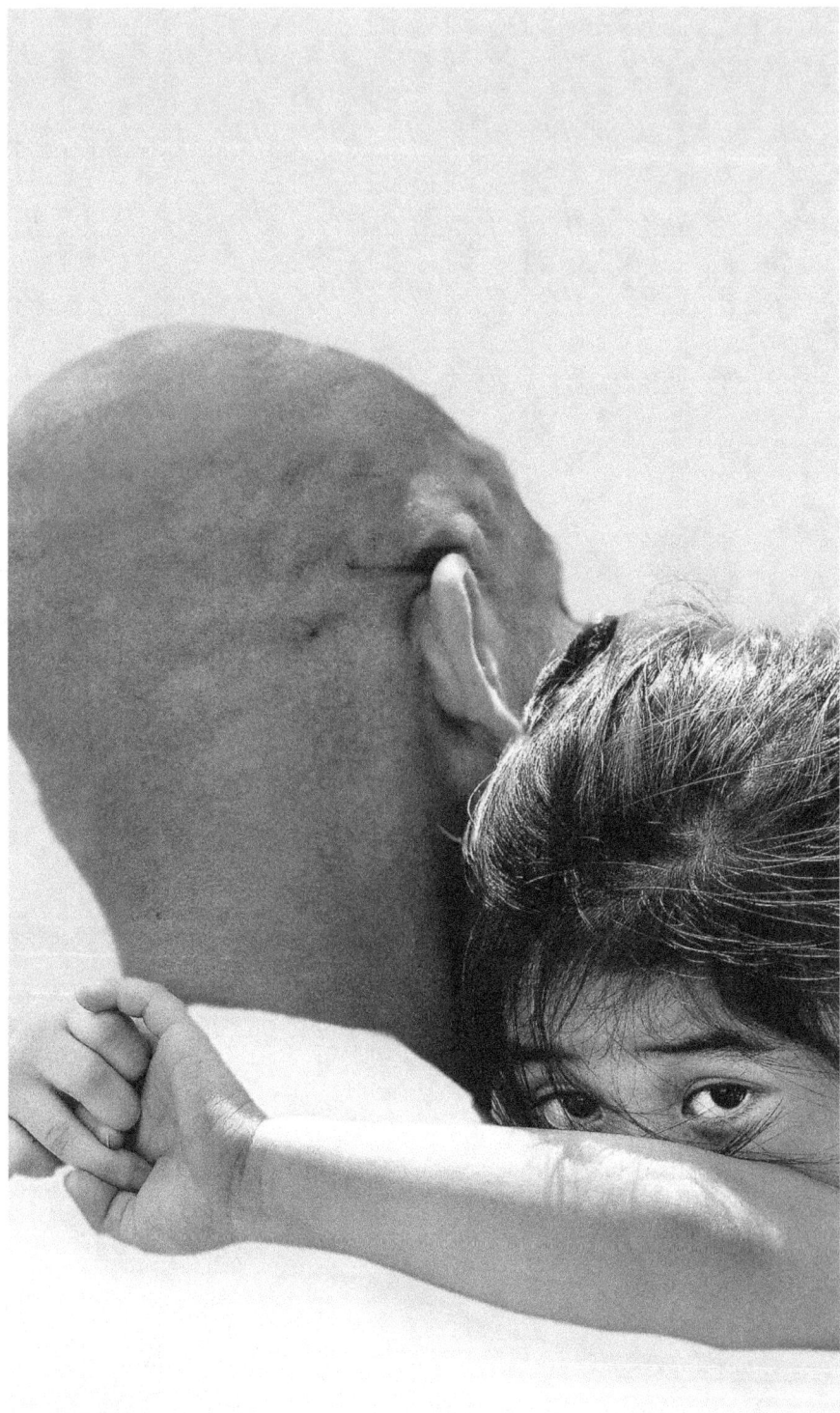

The Journey – Part 4

Held Captive

To Set the Prisoners Free

Free, Free at Last

In the Embrace of Love

Romans 8:38-39

*For I am persuaded, that neither death, nor life,
nor angels, nor principalities, nor powers,
nor things present, nor things to come,
nor height, nor depth, nor any other creature,
shall be able to separate us from the love of God,
which is in Christ Jesus our Lord.*

87

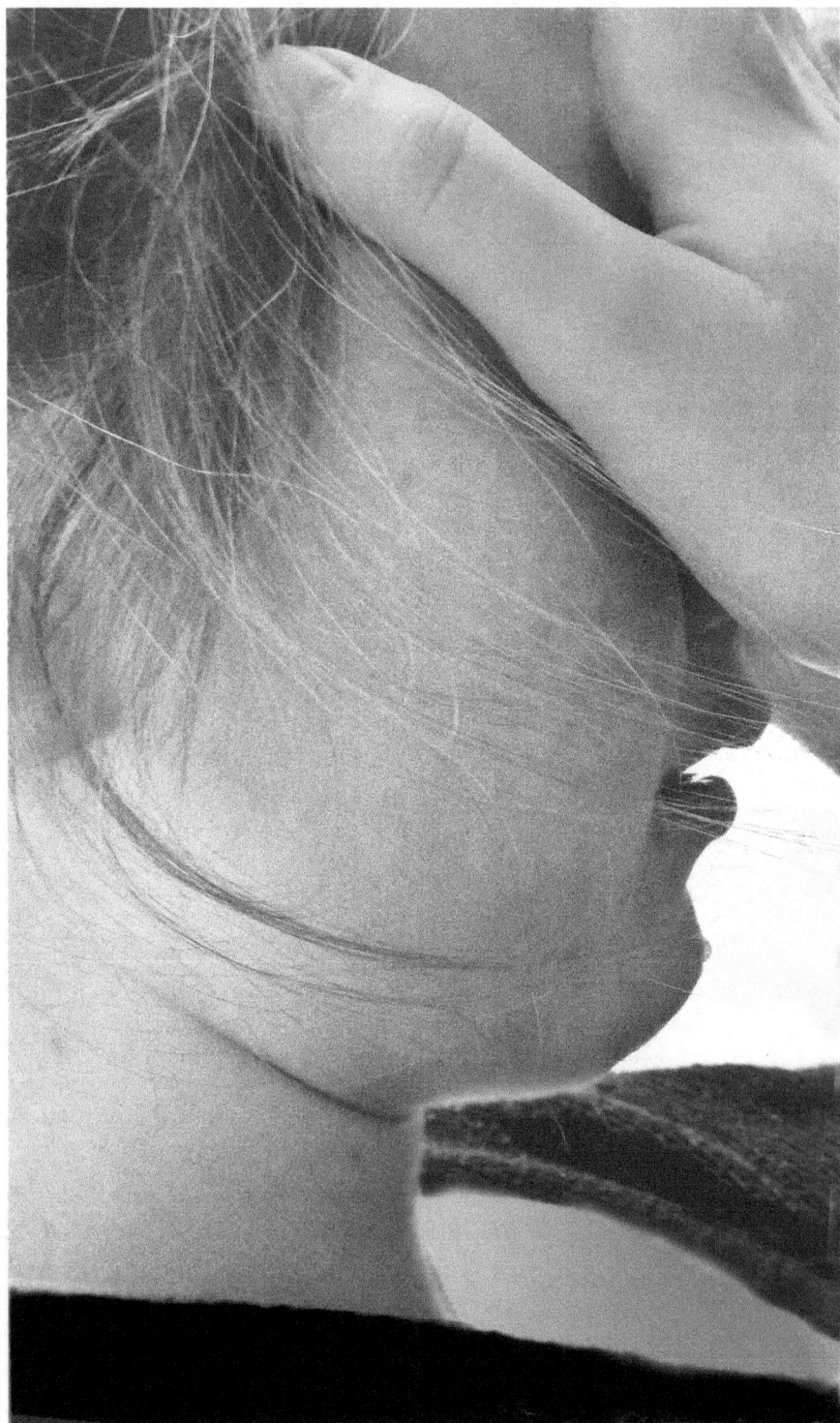

9

The God Who Weeps

Mary

John 11:1-45

Her beloved brother was dead. If only Jesus had been here. She knew Jesus loved him, but he did not come in time. Oh, why did he let his dear friend Lazarus die?

Many had loved Lazarus. He loved people, and this radiated throughout his life. Lazarus wanted to follow Jesus but needed to stay home. He was the only heir. He would soon be the man of the house and needed to care for his two sisters. But Jesus came often. He loved the comfort of their house, and Lazarus seemed to bring special joy to Jesus. Lazarus longed to just be with Jesus, to sit, to listen. Why did Jesus not come before it was too late? Why? Why? Why?

Surely he had heard by now. Why did he not come? Others came. For four days they had come. For four days Mary had stayed alone weeping.

Suddenly she heard commotion in the main room. Martha came into her room breathlessly. "Mary. Mary, Jesus is here. He is asking for you."

A new hope rose in her heart. She got up and ran past all of the mourners. She ran as fast as she could to the tomb, only to find the tomb just as it had been for four days. Sealed shut. Her brother inside, dead. Her last flicker of hope died.

She fled up the path to where Jesus was walking. Seeing him, she fell sobbing at his feet. Finally in anguish she asked the question that had haunted her the last four days, "Lord, where were you? If you had been here my brother would not have died. Lord, why didn't you prevent this from happening?"

Jesus knelt down and lifted Mary to her feet and held her, weeping uncontrollably in his arms. He looked around at the others at the tomb, their tears, their sorrow. "Where have you laid him?" he asked gently.

"Come and see, Lord," said one of his disciples.

They slowly made their way to the tomb.

Mary wept uncontrollably, mumbling softly, "If only you had been here, Lord." Jesus looked down at her and around at the others, waiting, grieving, asking the same question.

For others, bitterness was already setting in and they directed their anger toward Jesus, "Could not this man who opened the eyes of the blind man have prevented this man from dying? Didn't he care! Where was he when we needed him?"

Jesus looked at the pain and anguish, knowing the questions in their hearts. And then Jesus wept.

Where were you? The question that echoed off the stone sealing the tomb. Silence.

Where were you, God? Where were you when the drunk driver killed my son? Where were you when my child died? Where were you God when my boy was kidnapped and murdered? Where were you when we lost our home, our village, our friends? Where were you when evil men invaded our home? Where were you, God?

Isn't that the question we want to shout at God? Where were you? Where were you when evil entered my world? But we're afraid to ask. Our religious system doesn't allow us to yell at God, to get really angry at Him. Secretly we think if we ask, if we get really mad at God, He will strike back.

But we want to ask. We want to know why. Why, if God is so powerful, did He allow this to happen? Doesn't He see? Doesn't He care?

Finally I had to ask. It was in the middle of the mountains, alone, sitting on a rock next to a lake, the full moon dancing off the water. I had sat weeping for hours as memories flooded back. Finally I had to know. In agony I shouted at God, "Where were you then?"

I was startled by the silence. Nothing. No answer. I had expected some sort of answer. Some comfort, that, perhaps Jesus was beside me, at my side during those moments of pain. But nothing. No answer. For the first time in my life God did not answer me. Silence.

Where were you? The question went unanswered. The question met with silence. In the moment I needed God the most, in the moment my heart was longing to know some reason, some comfort for my pain, some good that would come from evil, He remained silent.

But as I sat bewildered, hurt, disappointed, another scene came to my mind. He hung on the cross. Beaten, humiliated, naked. Alone in darkness. Racked by pain, Jesus cried out in a loud voice, *"Eloi, Eloi, lama sabachthani?"* My God, my God, why have you forsaken me?

The Son of God cried out to his Father, "God, where are you now?" And there was silence. For the first time in his life, his Father did not answer him. Nothing. Silence echoed throughout the heavens.

In the moment of Jesus' greatest need, God turned his back. In the moment that His son was carrying the sins of the world, the God of truth turned his back. His own father did not answer him. Silence.

But as God turned His face from the one He loved, there were tears. As His son cried out in agony, God wept.

God wept!

God was there. But He did not intervene. He did not stop evil men from doing what they wanted to His Son. He does not stop evil people now. He hates it. He will judge them, but He has given people free will. To love or to hate. To do good or to do evil. But God is there!

There will be a time when every tear will be gone, every heartache will be healed. But for now disease, disasters, death are part of our fallen world. Not a part of the world God intended. But God is there.

In your moment of pain, God was there.

In the moment your life was shattered, God cared.

In the moment you cried out in anguish, God wept.

Reflection Questions
Chapter 9 - The God Who Weeps

1. When have you felt that God did not care?

2. When have you felt angry with God? What did you do?

3. When have you felt that God was silent and did not answer your prayers?

4. What do you think would happen if you expressed your real feelings to God?

5. How do you think God feels when people do evil things?

6. How would your perspective change if you knew God was with you and wept with you?

10
Abandoning Ourselves to Love

Martha

John 11:1-45

Lazarus' fever still soared. He had been sick for a week, and the fever would not go down. The doctors had tried everything they could, but there was no longer much hope. Lazarus' health declined too far, too fast.

Martha called a servant to her. "Go find Jesus. Tell him that Lazarus…no, tell him that the one he loves is sick. Hurry! I know he'll come as soon as he hears. He won't let his friend die. He has healed others. He can heal Lazarus, too."

The servant went quickly. After two days of travel, he finally found where Jesus was staying. Immediately Jesus recognized him as one of Martha's servants. Exhausted, the man knelt at Jesus' feet. "Lord," said the servant, "Lord, the one you love is sick."

When he heard this, Jesus said, "This sickness will not end in death. No, through it people will see God's power."

Reluctantly the disciples began making preparations to go to Bethany. They feared what would happen if Jesus traveled so close to Jerusalem. The authorities had everyone looking for Jesus. They would not let him escape this time.

Yet they knew how much Jesus loved Martha, Mary, and Lazarus. How many happy, peaceful days he had spent at their home. He would not turn down their urgent request. So they packed up their things and waited. And waited. And waited. Each day wondering why Jesus did not leave yet. Each day more relieved that he was not going.

As soon as Martha sent the servant to find Jesus, Lazarus had slipped into a coma. On the second day his sickness ended in death. Lazarus was dead.

Mourners came from all around. Lazarus with his joyful spirit and easygoing nature was a favorite with everyone. Many came out of respect for Martha and Mary.

But Martha waited for just one. And she waited, hoping, thinking perhaps he would come soon. They would not bury Lazarus as long as there was hope.

But as night fell, the flicker of hope died. They could delay burial no longer. They placed Lazarus in the family tomb. The stone sealed the tomb. Jesus had not come. Lazarus was not saved. Death stung with finality. It was too late.

The days were a blur for Martha as visitors came and went. She kept herself busy instructing her servants in food preparations and caring for her guests. But the thought, the question in her mind was, "Where was he? If he had come when I asked, this would never have happened. Lazarus would still be alive."

Suddenly one of the servants rushed in, "Jesus is on his way." As soon as she heard, Martha quickly ran out to meet Jesus.

Before she could stop herself, Martha blurted out the question that had been on her heart the past four days, "Lord, if you had been here, my brother would not have died. If you had come when I asked, he would still be alive." Suddenly she was ashamed. Who was she to accuse the Lord?

Looking into Jesus' eyes, she did not see anger but love. Love that caused a flicker of hope to be reignited. Love that asked her to trust. Yet she was too afraid to dare to hope, yet wanting to. Timidly she said, "But I know that even now God will grant you whatever you ask."

Jesus knew the question she wanted to ask, the request she was afraid to make. He announced, "Your brother will rise again."

Martha looked into Jesus' eyes searching, wanting to believe, yet not able to. She knew the right answer. She had heard it since childhood, "I know he will rise again in the resurrection at the last day."

Jesus paused, patiently wanting this person whom he loved so much to believe him, in him. Not just to give the right answers, but to know the Answer. To know him, not just about him, not just the things he did, but to know, truly know who he was. How he wanted to reveal himself to her if she would only believe.

"Martha," Jesus said gently, "I am the one who raises people from the dead. I am the one who gives eternal life. Anyone who believes in me, even though he dies will live again. And whoever believes in me will have eternal life. This is who I am. Do you believe this?"

Martha stood, trying to absorb this. She wanted to believe, to trust, but she could not stretch that far. She could not let go. She answered with the right response, "Yes, Lord, I believe that you are the Christ, the Son of God who was to come into the world."

She could not stay any longer. She quickly went back to the house, weeping. Why could she not believe? Why could she not let go and just believe in him? She longed for the relationship that Mary had with him. Mary knew him. Martha still only knew about him. Martha wiped her tears and went in and called Mary.

As she walked slowly back to the tomb, her thoughts were on him. His love. She had spent days serving him, but she did not truly know him. She knew all the right answers. But he was asking her to step into the unknown. To believe what she could not see, what she could not understand.

She came to the tomb and saw Jesus approach, weeping with Mary at his side. Suddenly Martha found something melting her heart. He came to her and looked deeply into her eyes, drawing her, entreating her to believe. "Martha, take away the stone."

Without thinking she blurted out, "But, Lord, he's been in there four days. There is no more hope. His body has already begun to decompose."

Jesus continued to look deeply into Martha's eyes, "Didn't I tell you that if you believed you would see the glory of God?"

They stood looking into each other's eyes. Martha tottering between faith and doubt. Between knowledge and faith. His will or her will? Trust herself or trust his love? Jesus waiting, drawing her toward him.

Keeping her eyes upon him, she, for the first time in her life, stepped into the unknown.

Martha, the practical, did the absurd. Martha let go and abandoned herself to his love. To her servants waiting nearby she said, "Take away the stone."

We can spend years following Jesus. We can spend years knowing about Jesus. But there comes a point when we have to trust, to abandon ourselves to his love. We step beyond what we know, what we have seen, what is beyond the scope of our experience. Doing things that don't seem to make sense.

But God seems to make a point of asking people to do that. In fact He even seems to take delight in asking us to believe the absurd.

Do you realize how preposterous it must have sounded when God told Abraham that he would be the father of nations when he didn't even have a son? Don't blame Sarah for laughing. We probably would have laughed, too.

Or can you imagine Moses? Pharaoh's army behind, the Red Sea in front.

Or David, standing before a giant with nothing more than five stones and a lot of faith?

Or Ruth with no husband, no hope? Only knowing she wanted to know this God who Naomi worshiped.

Who would have imagined she would be great-grandmother to a king?

Or think about Mary. Can you imagine how absurd it sounded when she told Joseph that she was pregnant—and the father was God?

Sometimes God brings us an impossible situation so that we finally have to abandon ourselves to His love.

But maybe for you, it isn't an impossible situation you are facing. Perhaps the impossible is believing what He already knows about you. Perhaps He is asking you to believe that He really loves you. He thinks you are beautiful no matter what your world has taught you. That God will give you good gifts, not ones you think you need but ones that you really need. That the God of the universe actually enjoys being with you and desires to have a relationship with you.

Sound absurd? As absurd as Jesus raising a man four days in a tomb? There are times when we just have to believe. We have to make a choice. We must choose between holding onto self-hate or accepting another's love. We have to let go of what we have known our whole lifetime and believe something new. Something that we cannot really imagine. Something that is totally outside of our experience. We have to abandon ourselves to the One who loves us. To finally let go. And when we do, God will surprise us beyond our wildest dreams.

Oh, and the end of our story? The absurd became reality. The brother who had died, the brother who had been wrapped in graveclothes, the brother who had been in the tomb four days, the brother they thought they had lost forever? He came walking out of the tomb into their arms. Jesus surprised them beyond their wildest dreams.

Reflection Questions
Chapter 10 - Abandoning Ourselves to Love

1. What things in your life do you think are impossible for God to change?

2. What prevents you from believing God can do these things?

3. What things about yourself do you have a hard time believing?

4. What are some things about God you have a hard time believing?

5. What keeps you from fully surrendering to His love?

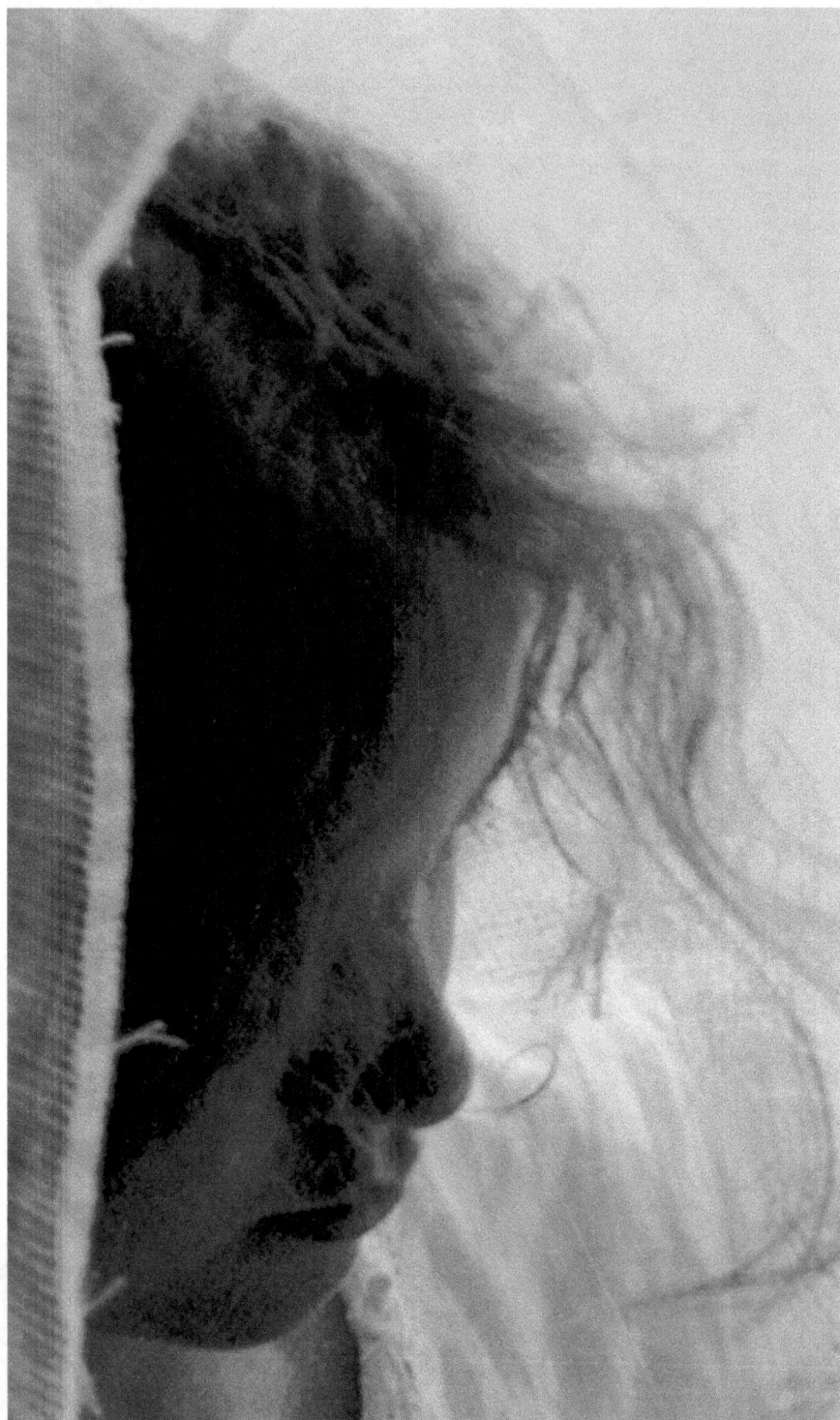

11

Invitation to Love

Mary

John 12:1-9

─────────────────

Mary sat at Jesus' feet as he and his disciples enjoyed the feast Martha had prepared. She gazed at Lazarus, laughing, joking with Jesus. Lazarus was alive. How her heart was filled with gratitude. She looked at Jesus, who was enjoying the respite from the crowds. At home with his friends again. What a wonderful gift Martha had given him. Her gratitude was shown in every dish.

How she envied Martha at this moment to have the talent and gifts to show her gratefulness in such a beautiful way. A feast in Jesus' honor. She looked at her sister as she moved gracefully among the men, gently directing the servants.

What a transformation had taken place. Martha served, but there was a new serenity. Martha truly served out of love and gratitude, using her gifts to honor Jesus.

But what could she do? Her heart was bursting with thankfulness. Her brother was alive. But she had nothing she could give.

As she looked upon Jesus' face again, she saw a shadow of sorrow behind his smile. A shiver went up her spine. There was something in his eyes that caused her to want to reach out and comfort him. A great burden seemed to be weighing on his heart.

Then she remembered and knew what she must do. The alabaster bottle with the perfume. It was her inheritance, her security, her future. It was all she had. It was her gift.

She quickly got up and ran back to her room. There it was—the sealed bottle. She stood holding it for a moment, admiring the pattern. The slender neck was sealed. It could only be opened by breaking the neck. If she were to give this, she would give it all.

None of this mattered as she ran back to the room where the men were reclining. She broke open the bottle, and its scent filled the air. She poured the perfume, joyfully, completely, on Jesus' feet. Then with a grateful heart she wiped his feet with her hair. Tears mingled with the perfume. Joyful in her brother's return, she knew somehow that Jesus would soon be leaving. Joy and pain were mixed together in her tears.

Jesus looked at her with love and sorrow, knowing the events that were about to take place. He knew the pain that was ahead for them. He knew how hard it was to say good-bye.

Intuitively Mary knew this was goodbye. Her sensitive heart had picked up all his references to his death. And she knew that his death was imminent. His eyes met hers, and she understood.

The disciples were shocked into silence. Mary had gone too far. They did not mind her sitting listening, but this time she had gone too far. Look at the waste. They all knew the cost of the perfume. Surely the Lord would not approve of such a wasteful extravagance.

Then Judas spoke up, "What a waste. She could have given us the perfume, and we could have sold it and given the money to the poor." The other disciples silently agreed.

Jesus' eyes flashed with anger. He knew Judas did not say this because he cared for the poor. He replied, "Leave her alone. She did this in preparation for my death. The poor you will have with you always. But I am not going to be with you much longer."

Mary and Judas. What a contrast. One gave to Jesus. The other stole from him. One loved Jesus, the other betrayed him. One is famous for her love. The other famous for his death. Same invitation. Two different responses.

What made the difference? Did Jesus love Mary and not Judas? Actually Jesus probably spent more time with Judas and right to the end offered him love and friendship. So what made the difference? Did Jesus not love both of them? Yes, he did. He gave them both the same invitation. One said yes. The other said no.

God longs to love us. But we cannot experience his love unless we want to receive it. So many times we focus on what we have to do for God. What we have to give up. Our religion is defined in terms of duty, doing the right things at the right times in the right way. But Jesus does not offer us religion. He offers himself. He offers us a relationship. He offers us his love. But we have to accept it to finally receive it.

Two people. Two responses to an invitation to love. Jesus is waiting. He has already shown how much he loves you. He died not for your sacrifice, not for your duty, but for you. Think about it. The God of heaven and earth wants to have a relationship with you. The God of love wants you to experience His love for you. His invitation is waiting for your response. Love or duty. Religion or relationship. It's up to you. You must decide.

Reflection Questions
Chapter 11 - Invitation to Love

1. What was the difference between Mary's and Judas' response to Jesus?

2. Have you experienced God's love for you?

3. Jesus' invitation for a relationship is waiting for you. What will be your response?

If you want to accept Jesus' invitation you only have to tell him. Prayer is just talking to God. You can say something like this:

Jesus I want to be transformed by your love. I want to know you and have a relationship with you. I have sinned and there are things in my life that are not pleasing to you. I want to know you as my Lord and Savior, the one who died for my sins so I can start a new life. I abandon myself to your love to begin a new life with you.
Amen

The Next Step

We love him, because he first loved us.

1 John 4:19

In a few moments we will go our separate ways again. I hope you have enjoyed meeting my friend Jesus as much as I have enjoyed introducing him.

I hope for those of you who have not yet begun your journey you have found courage to begin. It may be painful. It may be long. But Jesus does promise to be with you. He does care. He loves you. He promises that he will never abandon you, no matter what.

For those who began your journey long ago I hope you have been refreshed. Although it may seem like a slow process, God promises to continue His work in your life.

Thank you for joining me for a short time on my own journey. You have been a part of the fulfillment of God's promise to me. What people intended for evil, He will use for good.

I hope that your life will be transformed by love.

Reflection Questions
The Next Step

1. What single step can you take next on your journey?

2. In what ways has your life been transformed by love?

And this is the record, that God hath given to us eternal life, and this life is in his Son. He that hath the Son hath life; and he that hath not the Son of God hath not life.

These things have I written unto you that believe on the name of the Son of God; that ye may know that ye have eternal life, and that ye may believe on the name of the Son of God.

And this is the confidence that we have in him, that, if we ask any thing according to his will, he heareth us: And if we know that he hear us, whatsoever we ask, we know that we have the petitions that we desired of him.

1 John 5:11-15

Sources for Further Reading

Listed by Chapter

The narrations in this book touch on many issues and also briefly reference other stories that may be unfamiliar to you. Examining more extended accounts of the original stories can clarify the references, and also reveal further insights about being transformed by love. Here is a list of sources to aid in accessing references in the chapters.

An Invitation

[1] Hannah Hurnard. 1975. *Hinds' Feet on High Places.(pp. 25,27)* Wheaton: Tyndale House Publishers, Inc. This book is a delightful allegory about a journey of healing, transformation, and restoration. The quotes at the beginning of this book are from the start of the main character's journey.

On finding one's path, see Proverbs 3, especially verses 5 and 6.

1. The Fighter

The reference to "The Way" comes from John 14:5-7.

The story about Abraham pleading for Sodom is found in Genesis 18:16-33.

Moses asks God to show His glory in Exodus 33:12-23.

The story about Jacob is found in Genesis 32:22-32.

The story about Peter's failure is found in John 18:15-18 and John 18:25-27. His restoration is found in John 21:1-25.

2. When Dreams Die

The story of when the first family was shattered is told in Genesis 4:1-16.

The story of the Prodigal Son is told in Luke 15:11-32.

3. Shame Removed

The story about Moses killing an Egyptian is found in Exodus 2:11-14. A detailed account of how Moses led Israel out of Egypt is found in Exodus 2-15.

The story about David's sin and restoration is found in 2 Samuel 11:1-12:24.

Rahab's story is in Joshua 2:1-21.

Paul's transformation is found in Acts 9:1-31.

Stories about Paul's life as a missionary are found in Acts 11:19-30 and Acts 12:25-Acts 28:31.

4. Liberated by Love

Some other places that specifically mention women disciples:
Luke 23:27-Luke 24:12 at Jesus' trial, death, and resurrection
Luke 8:1-3 names some women who followed Jesus.

5. Encounter with Truth

Other references to Samaritans give additional insight into the
depth of hatred between the Jews and Samaritans. In Luke
10:25-37 Jesus' parable uses a Samaritan to bring focus on
God's standards for loving our neighbors.

6. Encounter with Grace

Peter's commission is found in John 21:1-25.

More about John Mark can be found in Acts 12:25-13:13,
Acts 15:36-41, 2 Timothy 4:11, Colossians 4:10, and Phile-
mon 1:24.

7. Freed to Love

Matthew 12:46-50 describes Jesus' disciples as those who do the
will of the Father.

Luke 18:9-14 contrasts the activities of a Pharisee and a tax collector, of someone who looked good in the eyes of the world
and someone who looked good in the eyes of Jesus.

8. Freed to Praise

One story of Jesus eating with a tax collector is in Luke 19:1-10.

The reference for "Come to me all you who are heavy laden" is Matthew 11:28-30.

The reference for abundant life is John 10:10.

9. The God Who Weeps

The story of Jesus' death is found in Matthew 27:45-56.

The story continues with his burial and resurrection in Matthew 27:57 through Matthew 28:1-8.

10. Abandoning Ourselves to Love

Other places Jesus talks about giving eternal life are in John 3:16 and John 17:1-3.

The story about God's promise to Abraham and Sarah is found in Genesis 18:1-15.

The story of the parting of the Red Sea is in Exodus 14:1-31.

The story about David and Goliath is in 1 Samuel 17:1-54.

Ruth's story is told in the book of Ruth.

Mary's story is told in Matthew 1:18-25.

11. Invitation to Love

The story of Judas' betrayal and death is told in Matthew 26:14-56 and Matthew 27:1-10.

Acknowledgments

This book was not written alone but rather in a community of fellow travelers.

I want to thank my husband for being my fellow traveler for the past 20 years. It has been an adventure of love, learning, and laughter.

I want to thank Médine Keener for meeting with me monthly and reading through the chapters with me. She gave me a fresh, global perspective on the challenges that women around the world face. Her experience and insights have greatly enriched this book.

Several people read preliminary drafts of this book and provided critiques and comments that inspired numerous changes.

I want to thank my colleague Dr. Craig Keener for reading a draft and making comments to improve the textual and historical narration of the text.

I want to thank Julie Tennent for providing editorial comments as well as her enthusiastic support of this project. Her encouragement is a gift that I greatly appreciate.

I also want to thank the group of women at Asbury Theological Seminary who met monthly to read through a draft of this book. Their comments and experiences provided insights that have been incorporated into the narratives.

To my life group, I can only say that it is fun to walk through life with you. Your willingness to make this book one of our Bible studies helped me envision how it can encourage the church.

I am so grateful that there are people like my dear friends Desiree LaChapelle and Nancy Hoffman. They have a gift and talent for details and proofreading. Without them, this book would never have come to fruition.

To many dear friends and mentors, I hope you can see the influence of your lives on me in this work. Your willingness to walk portions of my journey with me has brought joy and healing and love.

For ever, O Lord,
thy word is settled in heaven.

Thy word is a lamp unto my feet,
and a light unto my path.

Psalm 119:89,105

www.ingramcontent.com/pod-product-compliance
Lightning Source LLC
LaVergne TN
LVHW021350080426
835508LV00020B/2215